T0182644

INNER VERSES

PAM REHM

✳

INNER VERSES

✳

WAVE BOOKS

SEATTLE/NEW YORK

Published by Wave Books

www.wavepoetry.com

Copyright © 2024 by Pam Rehm

All rights reserved

Wave Books titles are distributed to the trade by

Consortium Book Sales and Distribution

Phone: 800-283-3572 / SAN 631-760X

Library of Congress Cataloging-in-Publication Data

Names: Rehm, Pam, 1967– author.

Title: Inner verses / Pam Rehm.

Description: First edition. | Seattle : Wave Books, 2024.

Identifiers: LCCN 2024009250 | ISBN 9798891060104 (paperback)

Subjects: LCGFT: Poetry.

Classification: LCC PS3568.E47618 I56 2024 |

DDC 811/.54–dc23/eng/20240301

LC record available at https://lccn.loc.gov/2024009250

Designed by Crisis

Printed in the United States of America

9 8 7 6 5 4 3 2 1

First Edition

Wave Books 119

ACKNOWLEDGMENTS: Thank you to the editors of
Aurochs, *Colorado Review*, *Luigi Ten Co*, *Oxford Poetry*,
and *The Volta*, where some of these poems first appeared.

for Nate and Cora

One eye sees, the other feels.

PAUL KLEE

INNER VERSES

CONFIRMATION

Wild birds form
distances
for a restless eye

They retain
then edify
the soul's longings

I have lived as of late
unpracticed

My faith essentially
eroded

I am possessed now
with duration

As there is no measurement
to the turning
of a leaf into soil

Being also descends
with a slowness

Innocently enough
to witness

This river
awakened by the morning sun

A vale of close light

A light incarnate

INTERNAL DISQUIET

Along the grassy path paralleling the silent river,
geese stalk tagging the rocks at low tide with
their wobbling gait, waiting for the goslings to
follow suit. They wade in and out, false starts
in pursuit of a bigger crumb, a gentler current.

Keep moving. All morning the path kept me moving.

Lingering over the sunrise or garbage left at low tide,
I am crushed by this vigilance.
Always crushed by the salutary effects of the
intimate fragileness of this world.

The undeniable pull
of passion
is impossible
to let go of

Quite in love
with
the comfort
of walking
the weather,

having attuned to the light
that grows deeper
into the day's fading,

This empty awareness
is beneficent

A pulsing of pulses

Listen
to the place

Embrace
a weathered loneliness

Outdoorsy through the moss
and quietness

of colors
before spring's beginnings

Always one
passivity or another

guides the eyes

Raises an answer
to an incorporeal
question

absorbs a difficulty

creates a material world
intrinsic, but not reducible
to understanding

I have an indistinct
recollection

Lost the moment
I open my eyes

Times you might
know no goodbye

was ever walked through

Then it comes to you

Different and new

This image
in a rain puddle
quivering

Living is valiant. But
disastrous in its fusion
of sadness with vitality.
Yearnings are dear enough, then,
the "I" finds itself thwarted
by the vicissitudes of a loss.
Like a name drawn in sand
an alliance has gone missing.
Now a ghost haunts the kitchen
like a fragment of memory
walking backwards
into a photograph. Where
life commemorated life,
slow steps remain. The
ideal day. Kindred with
bluebells. A bird-soul, trembling.

BLEAK REALITIES

If you stand
in the gone sense
of stillness

These days
scatter goodness
too often

Uncertainty gives body
to the measuring
of everything

To which every part
and particle
risks meaninglessness

We live in a succession
of reflections

rooted in bankrupt emblems

I often feel we have lost
the will or the vision

at times

If words were true
If words come true

Then language will
resemble shelter

Open one eye
at a time

This onward prick
Ticking the mind by

A trick to justify
what we find
worth gleaning

Which of us is
perfect and fully winged?

I have no truck
with such a creature

but lose feathers
and settle groundward

You have to reconcile
Yourself with yourself

Continuously

No growth is final
Only initial

Not to the house
My attachment

But the trees
of birdsong
out back
of night fears

These slow
dawn reveries
have saved me

every time

GIVING UP REASON

It happens like this:

Majestically,
the pigeons spill down

a few steps away
on a hot summer's day
on Broadway

jostling one another
All the dust and the mess

I've become
overtaken

by unevenness
Within the days

Between the hours

I'm bewildered by
all the dollars I've spent

on a life out of balance
when there's all this

cosmic consciousness

within a kiss
and the I AM

that haunts the hand
in my pocket

searching for the key
hole

All those mistakes ago

Like everyone else,
I feed them

A few cents of bread
But it's the thirst

no one thinks about
When I look out

YOU are
always
The landscape within

How do you register
a life

gone out
Nothing properly ends

But is re-destined

Rudiments of encounter
Then parting

Always en route
to refinement

One becomes less and less
haunted

by living

By the days before one
By what time remains

The body is a conduit

And grace
its divine distillation

A CONSTRUCTION

for Keith Waldrop

A relationship is the
flux that binds

the tentative directions
the mind pulls together

An adept sense
at finding other

affinities,
intimacies

A man casts off his knowledge
as he casts off

his calendar body
A worn bargaining

The underneath mind
growing more and more
quieted

By liminal attachments
By a self-gathered credo

As the remedial force

The poet is transfixed by
what is not

apparent
Beneath notice

The internal dialogue
Ecstasy or torture?

In the beginning
A gamble

Wisdom or desire?

Crossing a commons
The snow at twilight

These silences written
within the mind

imposter gods
Take account

You are your own
Ghost

"ALL THAT LIFE EVOKES"

for Steven

All that life evokes
at any given moment
time congeals

A hero's halo
The bitter feeling
touching the heart's peace

There's no consolation for
how precariously we live
inside of fictions

Under pressure of necessity
from anxiety's quivers
The body sketches out
the suppliant it has become

Running the risk
Of living, again—
once the possibility

possesses you like hunger—
is its own drug

Sometimes destiny will be kind
and second chances will feel like valor

Endeavor to find that reflection
In your own armor

ADORATION

The heart can break
open

in a camouflaging
self-erasure

It happens
almost abruptly

In a brief intimacy
with the shifting

browns
of winter's branches

or the side-eyed reproach
of a winged predator

❋

In a heart
What is held

opened

Slowly
The days lengthen

Out of the caterpillar's
pupal sleep

The brevity of life
holds

our shape
Heart-strung

Along
An intimately
shifting
Length of day

I was not sure how
my children would dream

They saw further
than sheltering

They heard clearer
than any prayer

I could not feel my rescue
Intently enough

They held me tighter
than any grip

They led me across
my indigence

and were my abundance
when I got there

Sprung up like wild herbs

I had always hoped
To find

GETTING THE WOLF OUT

for Tirzah Goldenberg

How is the dream formed—

At the edge of the visible?

Within a shattering
  and joining back together?

The person does not really change

It is the discovery
  of the threats to it

of what eats at the heart's
  tenderness

You heard the forlorn sounds
  of late birds singing

You opened the door
  to a tempest of snow

A rational soul
   You were led by your desire for home

Haunted by the boundaries
   of a continuum

by all the shadows
   that still remain

GIVE-AND-TAKE

for Rosmarie Waldrop

A handful of sense takes
The edge off uncertainty's
Infinite tremblings. A sense

the hand has giving pleasure
or the ardor of a lover
takes a great deal of

composure. What you
put your faith in
gives modest hope.

The pulse of second by
second. Gulls cruising
overhead. What does it

take to give, inexorably
into. Absolving oneself.
A poet's tongue

wooing the depths. A truth-hunger.
An inner versing. Once upon once.
That's the way. Desire takes you.

WHAT CANNOT BE

for Charles Bernstein

What cannot be eaten is called discretion
What cannot be squandered is called patience
What cannot be cultivated is called intuition
What cannot be chastened is called longing
What cannot be renounced is called affection
What cannot be rectified is called regret
What cannot be defeated is called aging
What cannot be confronted is called ritual
What cannot be helped is called personal
What cannot be reconciled is called memory
What cannot be registered is called loss
What cannot be evaded is called aftermath
What cannot be promised is called vision
What cannot be mastered is called heartache

5 / 3 0 / 9 6

for Chris Stroffolino

It won't always be a high tide
that you need to cover up the debris
that got left behind when the last wave
was a goodbye that never really made it
and is back again sooner than the sun
you can't hide under a bucket
to keep from getting burned
When you are this desert island,
I will be your tree,
not romantically or momentarily
but uncompromisingly
So that what seems like isolation
is only the appearance
you make of yourself
Or the mirror's exaggeration
of your bed at night as you lie up,
listening, intent on what
you can't imagine love would mean

if you were the loved one
instead of the one who loves,
like one who prays,
into the sky above

HYMN TO CONVALESCENCE

The year is all but
shut

Here
bare winter trees

To work out
Mortality

Inimically

Outside the vicissitudes
of this world

Inside
Time's slow quickening

This is what leaves you
against yourself

The soil of the self
falling out

What is your innermost
reassurance

What is your most
intimate intimacy

What is it
That walking settles out

*

Memory's many dimensions
Startle

A continuous permission
To be permitted to return

to those whom we love
like migrating birds

moving behind the darkness

Settling out a horizon
Indefinitely

Outside of Paradise

The unspeakable reaches
of things hoped for

Leave a disfiguring
Interiority

But it is not this sadness
of a missing
touch

But a full-blown admission
that disenchantment will be infinite

Deep winds quicken
Reading echoes walking

There is no need
called quickness

There is only a deep
needing

to be attentive to everything

Feelings are always inextricable
companions

They measure the long shadows

Of coming to terms with
keeping

time together

By the waters of the Hudson
I stand up

looking forward to the merging
of this year with the

next
one's perplexities

I'm hedging my bets
against

the darkest shadows
of skepticism

BOWING TO FORCES INFINITELY GREATER

Sometimes the margin
of error can be so small
no one sees it

Other times it's so large
it's televised

But most of the time,
it's on a scale
that's body-sized

One risks mortality
every day
as a spiritual exercise

We're caught in this trap

Of linear time
always getting tied
to perspective

Surely, a genuine devotion lapses

Today and tomorrow
quietly revolve
untutored

Caring for the self
consists of becoming
aware

as a psychological truth

Reverence for others
comes as naturally
as making the same mistake
again and again

Regret merely surrenders
self-cultivation

Confucius refused
to define definition

That is the beauty
in his teaching

The beauty of life
as ecstatic vision

Each word
a vigilance

"I hope"
fused to

its shadow
(sorrow)

Trees stripped
A haunting

The perceptible
And what we perceive

That difference
Dislocates

You know it
in your bones

Vitality in constant tension
with assurance

The puzzle of instinct
Startles
Intelligence

With the best thoughts
Already worrying

Standing within the body
often makes talking paralyzed

There is no parallel
just this puzzle

of orienting certainties
failing

where we are

If experience becomes
unsayable

At the deepest leveling
the mind's
these very wilds

it is lost
in its immediacy

There is no answer
that doesn't come

as a cost
to the body

The mind
desperately trying
to impose meaning

A painful diligence
A temperate grappling

that hews to everything
encroaching

on the body's pace

on the peace
I want to leave with you

I was holding on
to something

I thought was us
Fate or Providence

A sense of purpose
And the passion

of understanding

At heart

I don't know
How each part is connected

Eyes for seeing
Teeth for chewing

What then
Blind desires, insatiable greed

Loneliness for hire

Change and necessity
engage a certain solace

Remember this
Renewal is an age-old freedom
Despite friendship
Or the accompaniment of a god

Love and its absence
Move through us, moving us

How much sense we make
out of nothing but

an intricate tracing of how it feels
to be alive